Fractions Practice Ages 9–11

T0372048

Revision & Practice

KS2 Years 5–6

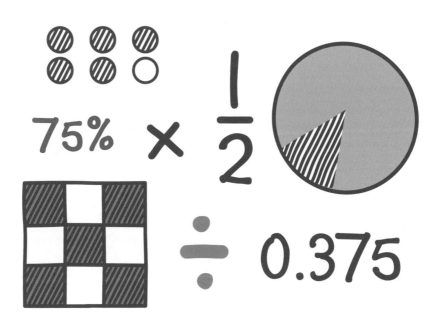

Build confidence with targeted skills practice

First published in the UK by Scholastic, 2020; this edition published 2024
Scholastic Distribution Centre, Bosworth Avenue, Tournament Fields, Warwick CV34 6UQ
Scholastic Ireland, 89E Lagan Road, Dublin Industrial Estate, Glasnevin, Dublin D11 HP5F

www.scholastic.co.uk

A CIP catalogue record for this book is available from the British Library.
ISBN 978-1407-18349-7

Printed by Leo Paper Products, China

The book is made of materials from well-managed,
FSC®-certified forests and other controlled sources.

Author Paul Hollin
Editorial team Rachel Morgan, Audrey Stokes, Robin Hunt, Kate Baxter, Tracy Kewley,
David and Jackie Link, Suzanne Holloway
Design team Dipa Mistry, Andrea Lewis, QBS Learning
Illustration Kevin Payne

Notes from the publisher

Please use this product in conjunction with the official specification and sample assessment
materials. Ask your teacher if you are unsure where to find them.

The marks and star ratings have been suggested by our subject experts, but they are to be used as
a guide only.

Answer space has been provided, but you may need to use additional paper for your workings.

Contents

The answers can be found online at:
www.scholastic.co.uk/sats-fractions

How to use this book

This book provides you with a step-by-step guide to all aspects of fractions, decimals and percentages, providing a complete route to mastery of this vital area of the National Curriculum for Mathematics at Key Stage 2.

Title – there are 12 units in total and two practice tests.

Recap what you should have learned already.

Practice what you have learned with arithmetic-style questions. NB some questions include a large answer box to show your workings.

Solve problems – these will be similar to those you may see in national tests.

Learn what you need to know to tackle the questions.

At the end of the book are two practice tests which provide questions similar to those you may see in national tests.

A handy progress chart on page 5 allows you to track your understanding. It is a good idea to only tick off a section when all of the questions have been completed correctly, with mistakes corrected and any misunderstandings clarified.

There is a useful glossary at the back of the book, and answers are available online at: **www.scholastic.co.uk/sats-fractions**

Progress chart

Making progress? Tick (✔) the circles as you complete each unit of the book.

Work through one unit at a time before moving on to the next one.

1 Identifying fractions ◯

2 Equivalent fractions ◯

3 ◯

4 Comparing and ordering fractions ◯

Adding and subtracting fractions ◯

5 Multiplying and dividing fractions ◯

6 Fraction and decimal equivalence ◯

7 ◯

Rounding decimals ◯

8 Comparing and ordering decimals ◯

9 ◯

Adding and subtracting decimals ◯

10 Multiplying and dividing decimals ◯

11 Fraction, decimal and percentage equivalence ◯

12 Using percentages ◯

13 ◯

Practice test 1 – Arithmetic ◯

14 Practice test 2 – Reasoning ◯

Well done!

1 Identifying fractions

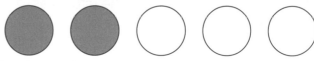

Two of these five dots are shaded.

We can use a **fraction** to tell us what **proportion** is shaded.

A fraction is a proportion of a whole.

It has a **numerator** on the top and a **denominator** on the bottom.

> Numerator ⟶ $\frac{2}{5}$
> Denominator ⟶

We say two fifths of the dots are shaded.
It means two out of five equal parts are shaded.

📋 Learn

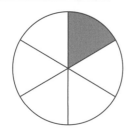

This circle is divided into six equal parts.

One whole is divided into six equal parts.

We say one out of six or one sixth $\frac{1}{6}$ has been shaded.

Notice that five parts have not been shaded. We say five sixths.

Two of the eight dots are circled.

We say two out of eight or two eighths $\frac{2}{8}$ are circled.

Six out of eight or six eighths $\frac{6}{8}$ are not circled.

Notice that we can **simplify** these fractions.

$\frac{1}{4}$ of the dots are circled, and $\frac{3}{4}$ are not.

> **To simplify a fraction:** Look for a common factor of the numerator and denominator. Here we can see that 2 is a common factor of 6 and 8. We divide the numerator and denominator by a common factor:
>
> $\frac{6 \div 2 = 3}{8 \div 2 = 4}$
>
> So, we can say that six eighths can be simplified to three quarters.

1. Shade the correct fraction of each shape.

a. $\frac{1}{2}$

b. $\frac{5}{8}$

c. $\frac{2}{5}$

d. $\frac{6}{9}$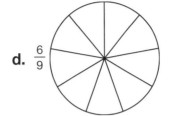

2. Write the fraction for the shaded dots in each set.

a.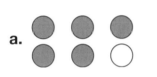

b.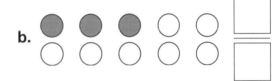

c.

d.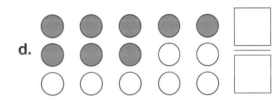

3. Write each fraction in words.

a. $\frac{1}{2}$ _____

b. $\frac{1}{6}$ _____

c. $\frac{3}{7}$ _____

d. $\frac{3}{8}$ _____

e. $\frac{1}{4}$ _____

f. $\frac{2}{3}$ _____

4. Write each fraction in numbers, using a numerator and denominator.

a. one sixth

b. four fifths

c. one third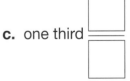

d. five twelfths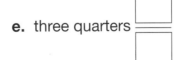

e. three quarters

f. two ninths

⚠ Solve problems

1. A baker has to put icing on 20 buns. Three buns must have pink icing, ten must have white icing, five must have blue icing, and the remainder must have red icing.

   Colour in the buns to help you.

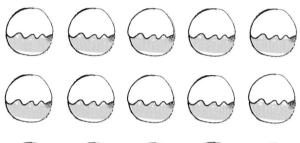

   a. Write the fraction for each colour of icing.

   pink: ⬜/20   white: ⬜/20

   blue: ⬜/20   red: ⬜/20

   b. Write the simplified fractions for white, blue and red.

   white: ⬜/⬜   blue: ⬜/⬜   red: ⬜/⬜

   c. If the baker sells nine buns, what fraction will be left over? ⬜/⬜

2. A classroom has 15 children in it.

   a. If eight of the children are boys, what fraction are girls? ⬜/⬜

   b. One more boy and two more girls arrive. Write the new fractions for each.

   girls: ⬜/⬜   boys: ⬜/⬜

   c. What fraction of the class are girls and what fraction are boys?

   _____

   _____

2 Equivalent fractions

↺ **Recap**

The **same proportion** can be shown by different fractions.

We can see from this circle that $\frac{3}{6}$ is the same as $\frac{1}{2}$.

We can say that three sixths is **equivalent** to a half.

A mixed number is a whole number and a fraction.

One whole can be written as a fraction with the same numerator and denominator.

$$1 \text{ whole} = \frac{2}{2} \text{ or } \frac{3}{3} \text{ or } \frac{10}{10} \text{ and so on.}$$

If the numerator is bigger than the denominator we call it an improper fraction.

$$\text{Mixed number} \longrightarrow 1\frac{1}{2} = \frac{3}{2} \longleftarrow \text{Improper fraction}$$

Learn

We can also use **common factors** to help us find equivalent fractions. Look:

$$\frac{3}{6} = \frac{1 \times 3}{2 \times 3}$$

We can see that 3 is a common factor of 3 and 6. If we divide the numerator and denominator by a common factor we can simplify the fraction.

$$\frac{3 \div 3}{6 \div 3} = \frac{1}{2}$$

So, we can say that three sixths is equivalent to one half.

We have simplified $\frac{3}{6}$ to get $\frac{1}{2}$.

This also works the other way. Here is $\frac{1}{5}$, with the numerator and denominator both multiplied by 4.

$$\frac{1 \times 4}{5 \times 4} = \frac{4}{20}$$

We can say that one fifth is equivalent to four twentieths.

Remember: We can multiply or divide the numerator and denominator by the same number without changing the size of the fraction.

✔ Practice

1. Draw a line to connect each fraction in the top row to its equivalent in the bottom row.

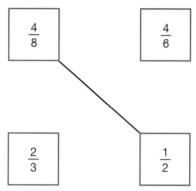

| $\frac{4}{8}$ | $\frac{4}{6}$ | $\frac{6}{10}$ | $\frac{9}{12}$ | $\frac{5}{15}$ |

| $\frac{2}{3}$ | $\frac{1}{2}$ | $\frac{1}{3}$ | $\frac{3}{4}$ | $\frac{3}{5}$ |

2. Write the fraction of each shaded shape, and then write it in its simplest form. The first one has been done for you.

$$\frac{2}{8} = \frac{1}{4}$$

a. 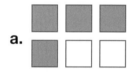 $\frac{\square}{\square} = \frac{\square}{\square}$

b.  $\frac{\square}{\square} = \frac{\square}{\square}$

c.  $\frac{\square}{\square} = \frac{\square}{\square}$

d. 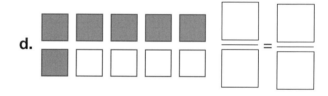 $\frac{\square}{\square} = \frac{\square}{\square}$

3. Change each of these improper fractions to a mixed number.

a. $\frac{4}{3} = \square\frac{\square}{\square}$

b. $\frac{6}{5} = \square\frac{\square}{\square}$

c. $\frac{13}{12} = \square\frac{\square}{\square}$

d. $\frac{7}{4} = \square\frac{\square}{\square}$

4. Change these mixed numbers to improper fractions.

a. $1\frac{4}{7} = \frac{\square}{\square}$

b. $2\frac{3}{5} = \frac{\square}{\square}$

c. $3\frac{5}{12} = \frac{\square}{\square}$

d. $5\frac{2}{5} = \frac{\square}{\square}$

⚠ Solve problems

1. Here are 12 shapes.

   Write the fraction for each group of shape, in its simplest form.

   circles: ☐/☐   squares: ☐/☐   triangles: ☐/☐

2. There are 15 chickens in a barn. Six of them are newly hatched chicks.

   a. What fraction of the birds are chicks? ☐/☐   Simplify this fraction: ☐/☐

   b. What fraction of the birds are not chicks? ☐/☐   Simplify this fraction: ☐/☐

3. Isaac has a bag of marbles. He says that one third of them are red, and counts nine red marbles.

   How many marbles are there altogether?

   _____ marbles

4. Amina asks 72 people to choose their favourite food from five options.

   Write fractions, in their simplest form, to show the proportion of people who choose each type of food.

Pizza	Pasta	Stir-fry	Salad	Chips
36	20	10	4	2
☐/☐	☐/☐	☐/☐	☐/☐	☐/☐

3 Comparing and ordering fractions

↻ Recap

We can change the numerator and denominator of a fraction while still keeping the same proportion.

$\frac{1}{2}$ is the same as $\frac{4}{8}$. We have multiplied the top and bottom by a common multiple (4).

Or we can divide the numerator and denominator by a common factor.

$\frac{6}{9}$ is the same as $\frac{2}{3}$. We have divided the numerator and denominator by 3.

📄 Learn

It is easier to **compare** fractions if they have the same denominators.

Which fraction is bigger, $\frac{1}{3}$ or $\frac{2}{5}$?

To answer this, we find the **lowest common multiple (LCM)** of the denominators and adjust each fraction.

Remember: Whatever you do to the bottom you must also do to the top.

The LCM of 3 and 5 is 15, so

$$\frac{1 \times 5 = 5}{3 \times 5 = 15} \text{ and } \frac{2 \times 3 = 6}{5 \times 3 = 15} \text{ so } \frac{1}{3} < \frac{2}{5}$$

Sometimes, one or both of the fractions can be simplified. For example, compare $\frac{7}{8}$ and $\frac{12}{16}$.

16 is double 8, so we can simplify $\frac{12}{13}$.

Remember:
= means equals
< means less than
> means greater than.

$$\frac{12 \div 2 = 6}{16 \div 2 = 8} \text{ so } \frac{7}{8} > \frac{12}{16}$$

✔ Practice

1. Convert each of these fractions to give them all a denominator of 12.

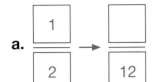 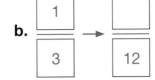 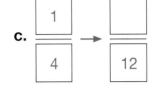

a. $\dfrac{1}{2} \rightarrow \dfrac{\square}{12}$ b. $\dfrac{1}{3} \rightarrow \dfrac{\square}{12}$ c. $\dfrac{1}{4} \rightarrow \dfrac{\square}{12}$

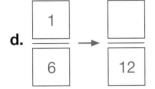 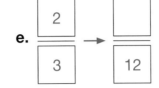 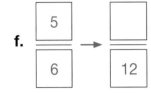

d. $\dfrac{1}{6} \rightarrow \dfrac{\square}{12}$ e. $\dfrac{2}{3} \rightarrow \dfrac{\square}{12}$ f. $\dfrac{5}{6} \rightarrow \dfrac{\square}{12}$

2. Write the original fractions in question 1 in order, from smallest to largest.

   The first one has been done for you.

$\dfrac{1}{6}$

3. Write the correct sign between each pair of fractions: >, < or =.

   a. $\dfrac{9}{21}$ $\square$ $\dfrac{3}{7}$ b. $\dfrac{3}{8}$ $\square$ $\dfrac{5}{12}$

   c. $\dfrac{3}{4}$ $\square$ $\dfrac{2}{3}$ d. $\dfrac{13}{3}$ $\square$ $4\dfrac{1}{5}$

4. Write these fractions in order from smallest to largest.

$\dfrac{4}{5}$ $\dfrac{19}{30}$ $\dfrac{5}{6}$ $\dfrac{7}{10}$ $\dfrac{11}{15}$

13

⚠ Solve problems

1. Lena says, " $\frac{7}{24}$ is greater than a quarter".

   Explain why she is right:

   _____

   _____

2. Hassan arranges fractions from smallest to largest. Shade the fraction that is in the wrong place.

   | $\frac{1}{4}$ | $\frac{3}{8}$ | $\frac{1}{2}$ | $\frac{5}{12}$ | $\frac{2}{3}$ | $\frac{3}{4}$ |

3. The table shows the fraction of girls in each class.

Class	Red	Blue	Green	Yellow
Fraction of children that are girls	$\frac{2}{3}$	$\frac{3}{4}$	$\frac{5}{8}$	$\frac{3}{6}$

   Write the class names in order, from smallest to largest, according to the fraction of girls in each class.

   _____   _____   _____   _____

4. Which is the largest fraction, $\frac{4}{3}$, $\frac{15}{12}$ or $\frac{18}{15}$?

   Explain your answer:

   _____

   _____

4 Adding and subtracting fractions

↺ Recap

We can count with fractions when the denominators are the same.

$$\frac{1}{10} + \frac{1}{10} + \frac{1}{10} = \frac{3}{10}$$

Notice that we **only add the numerators**.

We can also **subtract fractions** that have the **same denominator**.

$$\frac{3}{7} + \frac{2}{7} = \frac{5}{7}$$

$$\frac{7}{8} - \frac{4}{9} = \frac{3}{9}$$

Remember: It is only the numerators that we add or subtract.

📄 Learn

We can only add and subtract fractions if they have the same denominators.

Remember: Multiply the numerator and the denominator by the same number.

So, for the addition $\frac{2}{3} + \frac{1}{4}$

we find the lowest common multiple for 3 and 4, which is 12.

$$\frac{2 \times 4 = 8}{3 \times 4 = 12}$$ and $$\frac{1 \times 3 = 3}{4 \times 3 = 12}$$ So, the new addition is $$\frac{8}{12} + \frac{3}{12} = \frac{11}{12}$$

We can also add and subtract mixed numbers, as well as improper fractions.

$$3\frac{1}{2} - 2\frac{1}{4} = 1\frac{1}{4}$$

(Subtract the whole numbers first: $3 - 2 = 1$, and then the fractions $\frac{1}{2} - \frac{1}{4} = \frac{1}{4}$.)

$$\frac{5}{2} + \frac{4}{3} = \frac{15}{6} + \frac{8}{6} = \frac{23}{6}$$ (We can simplify this to $3\frac{5}{6}$: can you see how?)

✔ Practice

1. Add these fractions.

a. $\frac{1}{2} + \frac{1}{3} = \frac{\Box}{\Box}$

b. $\frac{1}{4} + \frac{1}{3} = \frac{\Box}{\Box}$

c. $\frac{1}{3} + \frac{1}{6} = \frac{\Box}{\Box}$

d. $\frac{1}{2} + \frac{2}{5} = \frac{\Box}{\Box}$

e. $\frac{1}{4} + \frac{3}{8} = \frac{\Box}{\Box}$

f. $\frac{1}{3} + \frac{4}{9} = \frac{\Box}{\Box}$

g. $\frac{1}{2} + \frac{1}{4} + \frac{1}{8} = \frac{\Box}{\Box}$

h. $\frac{1}{3} + \frac{2}{5} + \frac{3}{10} = \frac{\Box}{\Box}$

i. $\frac{2}{5} + \frac{3}{7} = \frac{\Box}{\Box}$

2. Subtract these fractions.

a. $\frac{1}{2} - \frac{1}{3} = \frac{\Box}{\Box}$

b. $\frac{1}{3} - \frac{1}{4} = \frac{\Box}{\Box}$

c. $\frac{1}{6} - \frac{1}{9} = \frac{\Box}{\Box}$

d. $\frac{2}{3} - \frac{3}{8} = \frac{\Box}{\Box}$

e. $\frac{5}{6} - \frac{1}{3} = \frac{\Box}{\Box}$

f. $\frac{3}{5} - \frac{1}{3} = \frac{\Box}{\Box}$

g. $\frac{4}{7} - \frac{2}{9} = \frac{\Box}{\Box}$

h. $\frac{11}{12} - \frac{3}{7} = \frac{\Box}{\Box}$

3. Find the answers.

a. $2\frac{1}{2} + 1\frac{1}{4} = \Box \frac{\Box}{\Box}$

b. $2\frac{1}{2} - 1\frac{1}{7} = \Box \frac{\Box}{\Box}$

c. $1\frac{1}{2} + \frac{1}{3} + \frac{1}{4} = \Box \frac{\Box}{\Box}$

d. $\frac{1}{4} + \frac{1}{6} - \frac{1}{8} = \frac{\Box}{\Box}$

e. $\frac{1}{3} + \frac{1}{9} + 1\frac{1}{2} = \Box \frac{\Box}{\Box}$

f. $\frac{5}{6} + \frac{3}{4} + \frac{7}{8} = \Box \frac{\Box}{\Box}$

g. $\frac{8}{15} - \frac{3}{8} = \frac{\Box}{\Box}$

⚠ Solve problems

1. Mia and Amy have a cake.

   They eat half of it on Monday, and one fifth of it on Tuesday.

   How much cake is left?

   $\dfrac{\boxed{}}{\boxed{}}$ of the cake

2. Josh's dad runs a pizza stall at a fair.

   One slice is one sixth of a pizza.

   At the end of the day he has sold $4\frac{1}{3}$ margherita

   and $3\frac{5}{6}$ vegetarian pizzas.

   How many pizzas has he sold altogether?

   $\boxed{}\dfrac{\boxed{}}{\boxed{}}$ pizzas

   PIZZA, ONLY
   £1 A SLICE!

3. A field has sheep in it.

   Half of the sheep are adult females.

   $\frac{1}{6}$ of the sheep are young females, and $\frac{1}{9}$ are young males.

   The rest are adult males.

   What fraction are adult males?

   $\dfrac{\boxed{}}{\boxed{}}$ are adult males

5 Multiplying and dividing fractions

↻ Recap

We can multiply fractions by whole numbers.

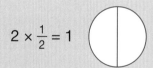 $2 \times \frac{1}{2} = 1$ two halves make a whole

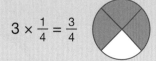 $3 \times \frac{1}{4} = \frac{3}{4}$

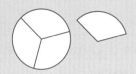 $4 \times \frac{1}{3} = \frac{4}{3} = 1\frac{1}{3}$

When we multiply fractions by whole numbers, we multiply the numerators together, and then the denominators together, for example,

$2 \times \frac{3}{7}$ can be written as $\frac{2}{1} \times \frac{3}{7} = \frac{6}{7}$.

Remember: We can write a whole number as a fraction with a denominator of 1, for example 2 can be written as $\frac{2}{1}$.

📄 Learn

We can **multiply one fraction by another fraction** using the same method.

$\frac{2}{3} \times \frac{4}{6} = \frac{2 \times 4}{3 \times 6}$ which equals $\frac{8}{18}$ which we can simplify to $\frac{4}{9}$.

When **multiplying mixed numbers**, first change them to improper fractions:

$1\frac{1}{3} \times \frac{5}{6} = \frac{4}{3} \times \frac{5}{6} = \frac{20}{18}$.   We can simplify this to $\frac{10}{9}$ or $1\frac{1}{9}$.

If you are asked to **divide a fraction** by a whole number, just multiply the denominator by the number.

$\frac{1}{4} \div 2 = \frac{1}{4} \times 2 = \frac{1}{8}$

It makes sense! A quarter of a cake shared between two people would give them an eighth each.

Give your answers in their simplest forms.

1. Multiply these fractions.

   a. $\dfrac{1}{2} \times \dfrac{1}{5} = \dfrac{\Box}{\Box}$

   b. $\dfrac{1}{4} \times \dfrac{1}{6} = \dfrac{\Box}{\Box}$

   c. $\dfrac{2}{3} \times \dfrac{3}{4} = \dfrac{\Box}{\Box}$

   d. $\dfrac{5}{8} \times \dfrac{2}{5} = \dfrac{\Box}{\Box}$

   e. $5 \times \dfrac{1}{3} = \dfrac{\Box}{\Box}$

   f. $8 \times \dfrac{3}{4} = \Box$

   g. $1\dfrac{1}{2} \times 4 - \Box$

   h. $1\dfrac{1}{2} \times 40 = \Box$

   i. $5\dfrac{1}{4} \times 16 = \Box$

2. Divide these fractions by whole numbers.

   a. $\dfrac{1}{2} \div 2 = \dfrac{\Box}{\Box}$

   b. $\dfrac{1}{3} \div 3 = \dfrac{\Box}{\Box}$

   c. $\dfrac{3}{8} \div 3 = \dfrac{\Box}{\Box}$

   d. $\dfrac{2}{3} \div 4 = \dfrac{\Box}{\Box}$

   e. $\dfrac{6}{7} \div 3 = \dfrac{\Box}{\Box}$

   f. $1\dfrac{1}{3} \div 2 = \dfrac{\Box}{\Box}$

   g. $2\dfrac{3}{5} \div 4 = \dfrac{\Box}{\Box}$

   h. $1\dfrac{2}{7} \div 3 = \dfrac{\Box}{\Box}$

3. Find the answers.

   a. $\dfrac{1}{4} \times \dfrac{8}{9} = \dfrac{\Box}{\Box}$

   b. $\dfrac{10}{11} \div 5 = \dfrac{\Box}{\Box}$

   c. $\dfrac{5}{6}$ of $600 = \Box$

   d. $\dfrac{4}{5} \times \dfrac{10}{12} = \dfrac{\Box}{\Box}$

   e. $\dfrac{11}{3} \div 6 = \dfrac{\Box}{\Box}$

   f. $\dfrac{2}{5} \times 180 = \Box$

   g. $4\dfrac{1}{2} \div 8 = \dfrac{\Box}{\Box}$

   h. $\dfrac{3}{7} \times 280 = \Box$

⚠ Solve problems

1. Which is more, $\frac{3}{4} \times \frac{2}{9}$ or $\frac{4}{5} \times \frac{3}{12}$?

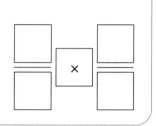

2. A tower is 120m high.

   A new tower is planned that is $1\frac{1}{3}$ times higher.

   What will be the height of the new tower?

   _____ m

3. Sonja takes a cake to school.

   To make sure everyone gets a slice, it is divided into eight equal slices, and then each of these slices is divided into three equal slices.

   What fraction of the whole cake is each slice?

   Each slice is ⬚⁄⬚

4. $\frac{3}{4}$ of the people at a concert are under 18.

   If 540 people are at the concert, how many of them are over 18?

   _____ people

6 Fraction and decimal equivalence

 Recap

Fractions show a proportion of a whole.

We write a fraction as a numerator over a denominator.

Decimals also show proportions of one whole.

They are written using tenths, hundredths and thousandths.

Numerator	$\longrightarrow$	$\frac{3}{8}$
Denominator	$\longrightarrow$	

0.375

So, 0.375 has 0 whole ones, 3 tenths,
7 hundredths and 5 thousandths.

Three tenths = $\frac{3}{10}$ or as a decimal 0.3

Seven hundredths = $\frac{7}{100}$ or 0.07

How would five thousandths be written as a fraction and a decimal?

Learn

We can change any fraction into its decimal equivalent by dividing the numerator by the denominator.

$\frac{1}{2}$ means one out of two, or 1 divided by 2.

To find out how to write this as a decimal, we can divide 1 by 2 using our usual division method.

So, $\frac{1}{2}$ = 0.5 (one half = zero point five).

2 goes into 1 zero times, with 1 carried over to the tenths column, then 2 goes into 10 five times.

$$2\overline{\smash)1.^10} \quad \begin{array}{c} 0.5 \end{array}$$

Try to follow the steps in this division to change $\frac{3}{4}$ to its decimal equivalent 0.75.

$$4\overline{\smash)3.^30\,^20} \quad \begin{array}{c} 0.75 \end{array}$$

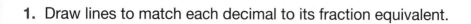

✔ Practice

1. Draw lines to match each decimal to its fraction equivalent.

| 0.5 | | 0.25 | | 0.2 | | 0.01 | | 0.1 |

| $\frac{1}{5}$ | | $\frac{1}{2}$ | | $\frac{1}{100}$ | | $\frac{1}{4}$ | | $\frac{1}{10}$ |

2. Draw lines to match each fraction to its decimal equivalent.

| $\frac{3}{4}$ | | $\frac{4}{10}$ | | $\frac{3}{5}$ | | $\frac{1}{8}$ | | $\frac{15}{100}$ |

| 0.6 | | 0.75 | | 0.4 | | 0.015 | | 0.125 |

3. Write T (true) or F (false) for each of these statements.

a. $\frac{1}{4} = 0.205$ ☐

b. $\frac{4}{5} = 0.8$ ☐

c. $\frac{6}{10} = 0.6$ ☐

d. $0.68 = \frac{68}{100}$ ☐

e. $0.875 = \frac{7}{8}$ ☐

f. $0.785 = \frac{6}{8}$ ☐

4. Calculate the decimal equivalents for these fractions.

a. $\frac{4}{5} =$ _____

b. $\frac{4}{10} =$ _____

c. $\frac{4}{100} =$ _____

d. $\frac{4}{20} =$ _____

e. $\frac{25}{100} =$ _____

f. $\frac{25}{50} =$ _____

g. $\frac{25}{10} =$ _____

h. $\frac{1}{3} =$ _____

i. $\frac{2}{3} =$ _____

⚠ Solve problems

1. Convert the fractions into decimals, then write these in their correct positions on the number line.

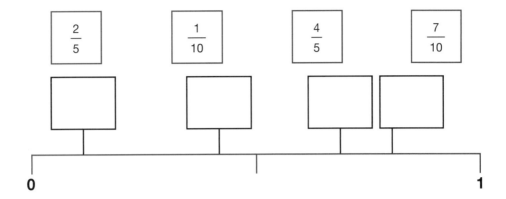

$$\frac{2}{5} \qquad \frac{1}{10} \qquad \frac{4}{5} \qquad \frac{7}{10}$$

0   1

2. Write the correct sign in each number sentence. Use < or >.

   a. $\frac{3}{4}$ ☐ 0.7

   b. $\frac{2}{7}$ ☐ 0.3

   c. $1\frac{1}{5}$ ☐ 1.5

3. Katrina says, "Seven eighths is equivalent to zero point seven eight five."

   Explain her mistake:

   _____

   _____

   _____

   _____

   _____

7 Rounding decimals

↻ Recap

Decimals show the fraction of one whole using tenths, hundredths and thousandths.

ones   tenths   thousandths

0.125

hundredths

So there are one hundred hundredths in one whole number!

Ten tenths make one whole.

Ten hundredths make one tenth.

And one thousand thousandths in one whole number!

Ten thousandths make one hundredth.

📄 Learn

Numbers are often rounded to the nearest whole number, or to the nearest tenth or hundredth. Look at these numbers between 2 and 3.

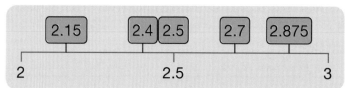

- Numbers less than 2.5 are nearer to 2; numbers above 2.5 are nearer to 3.
- Numbers below 2.5 **round down**. So 2.15 and 2.4 both round down to 2.
- Numbers above 2.5 **round up**. So 2.7 and 2.875 both round up to 3.
- As a special case, exactly 2.5 is rounded up, so 2.5 **rounds up** to 3.

We can also round hundredths up to tenths, and thousandths up to hundredths. So for example 0.36 rounds up to 0.4, and 0.384 rounds down to 0.38.

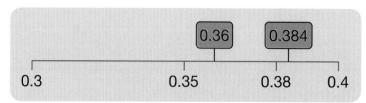

1. **a.** Write the correct words in these labels to show the place value.
   One is done for you.

   ones

   2.365

   b. Round the number to the nearest tenth: _____

2. Round each number to the nearest whole number.

   a. 4.3 = _____

   b. 2.8 = _____

   c. 5.48 = _____

   d. 0.6 = _____

   e. 3.5 = _____

   f. 0.2 = _____

   g. 7.45 = _____

   h. 4.634 = _____

   i. 1.52 = _____

3. Round each number to the nearest tenth.

   a. 4.327 = _____

   b. 8.86 = _____

   c. 7.25 = _____

   d. 6.38 = _____

   e. 0.23 = _____

   f. 12.48 = _____

   g. 1.541 = _____

   h. 2.65 = _____

   i. 0.03 = _____

4. Round each number to the nearest hundredth.

   a. 4.327 = _____

   b. 7.935 = _____

   c. 0.023 = _____

   d. 1.555 = _____

   e. 0.006 = _____

   f. 12.458 = _____

⚠ Solve problems

1. Circle the numbers that should be **rounded down** to the nearest whole number.

0.63   12.1   5.39

3.25   1.75   3.09

2. Round each number to the nearest tenth and to the nearest hundredth.

To the nearest tenth	Number	To the nearest hundredth
	3.752	
	0.067	
	12.245	

3. A shopkeeper decides to round everything she sells to the nearest pound (£).

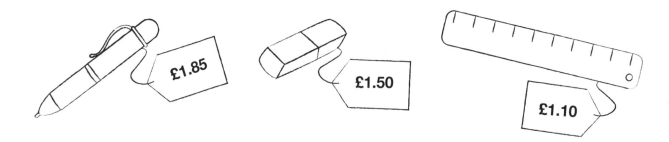

£1.85   £1.50   £1.10

    a. How much **more** will it cost to buy these three items after she has changed the prices?

> Pen new cost: _____ Eraser new cost: _____ Ruler new cost: _____

    b. Pencils cost £0.35 each. Explain why she cannot round the prices of pencils in the same way.

  _____

  _____

8 Comparing and ordering decimals

Decimals are fractions or tenths, hundredths and thousandths.

one whole = ten tenths

1 whole									
$\frac{1}{10}$	$\frac{1}{10}$	$\frac{1}{10}$	$\frac{1}{10}$	$\frac{1}{10}$	$\frac{1}{10}$	$\frac{1}{10}$	$\frac{1}{10}$	$\frac{1}{10}$	$\frac{1}{10}$

one tenth = ten hundredths

$\frac{1}{10}$									
$\frac{1}{100}$	$\frac{1}{100}$	$\frac{1}{100}$	$\frac{1}{100}$	$\frac{1}{100}$	$\frac{1}{100}$	$\frac{1}{100}$	$\frac{1}{100}$	$\frac{1}{100}$	$\frac{1}{100}$

one hundredth = ten thousandths

$\frac{1}{100}$									
$\frac{1}{1000}$	$\frac{1}{1000}$	$\frac{1}{1000}$	$\frac{1}{1000}$	$\frac{1}{1000}$	$\frac{1}{1000}$	$\frac{1}{1000}$	$\frac{1}{1000}$	$\frac{1}{1000}$	$\frac{1}{1000}$

📄 Learn

We can compare and order decimals more easily than fractions.

$\frac{3}{10} = 0.3$

3 tenths

$\frac{43}{100} = 0.43$

43 hundredths

$\frac{743}{1000} = 0.743$

743 thousandths

We can arrange these decimals on a number line:

We can also compare these decimals using inequality signs:

$0.43 > 0.3$ $0.743 > 0.43$ $0.3 < 0.743$

1. Mark and label each of these decimals in the correct position on the number line. You can use a ruler to help you. The first number has been done for you.

   a. | 0.3 | | 0.1 | | 0.8 | | 0.5 |

   b. | 0.27 | | 0.22 | | 0.25 | | 0.29 |

   c. | 0.563 | | 0.568 | | 0.561 | | 0.565 |

   (number line from 0.56 to 0.57)

2. Write the correct inequality sign in each statement, < or >.

   a. 0.308 ☐ 0.380   **b.** 0.763 ☐ 0.736

   c. 2.075 ☐ 2.121   **d.** 4.586 ☐ 4.6

1. Write these decimals in order from **smallest** to **largest**.

| 0.129 | 0.912 | 0.219 | 0.921 | 0.291 | 0.192 |

_____   _____   _____   _____   _____   _____

smallest   largest

2. Write a decimal in each empty box to make each statement true.

   a. 0.429 < [ ] < 0.442

   b. 0.35 > [ ] > 0.305

3. The decimals in this sequence increase by the same amount each time.

   Write the missing numbers.

   | [ ] | 0.325 | 0.435 | 0.545 | [ ] |

4. Jack says, "123 divided by 1000 is greater than 0.125"

   Explain his mistake:

   _____
   _____
   _____
   _____
   _____
   _____

9 Adding and subtracting decimals

Just as we can count with fractions, we can also count with decimals:

$$\frac{1}{10} + \frac{1}{10} + \frac{1}{10} = \frac{3}{10} \quad \text{and} \quad 0.1 + 0.1 + 0.1 = 0.3$$

$$\frac{1}{100} + \frac{1}{100} + \frac{1}{100} + \frac{1}{100} = \frac{1}{100} \quad \text{and} \quad 0.01 + 0.01 + 0.01 + 0.01 = 0.04$$

$$\frac{1}{1000} + \frac{1}{1000} = \frac{2}{1000} \quad \text{and} \quad 0.001 + 0.001 = 0.002$$

📑 Learn

Also, we can add decimals that have hundredths and thousandths.

$$\begin{array}{r} 0.372 \\ + \ 0.853 \\ \hline 1.225 \\ 1\ 1 \end{array}$$

Notice that we carry on tens to the next column, just like adding whole numbers because ten thousandths = one hundredth and ten tenths = one whole!

We can also subtract decimals, mentally or with written methods.

$$0.76 - 0.45 = 0.31$$

$$\begin{array}{r} {}^{1}{}^{1} \\ 3.6\ \cancel{2}\ 5 \\ - \ 1.2\ 1\ 8 \\ \hline 2.4\ 0\ 7 \end{array}$$

Notice how we borrow just like subtracting whole numbers.

✔ Practice

1. Add these decimals.

   a. 0.1 + 0.2 = _____

   b. 0.3 + 0.5 = _____

   c. 0.4 + 0.6 = _____

   d. 0.7 + 0.4 + 0.2 = _____

   e. 0.6 + 1.4 = _____

   f. 1.5 + 2.8 = _____

   g. 0.35 + 0.28 = _____

   h. 1.47 + 0.29 = _____

   i. 0.432 + 0.265 = _____

   j. 0.735 + 0.534 = _____

   k. 3.525 + 2.875 = _____

   l. 0.26 + 0.35 + 0.047 = _____

2. Subtract these decimals.

   a. 0.6 – 0.5 = _____

   b. 0.7 – 0.4 = _____

   c. 1.3 – 0.6 = _____

   d. 2.7 – 1.3 = _____

   e. 3.5 – 2.4 = _____

   f. 3.4 – 1.7 = _____

   g. 0.65 – 0.48 = _____

   h. 0.77 – 0.59 = _____

   i. 0.38 – 0.2 = _____

   j. 0.435 – 0.314 = _____

   k. 0.525 – 0.325 = _____

   l. 0.817 – 0.650 = _____

3. Find the answers.

   a. 0.62 + 0.37 = _____

   b. 0.62 – 0.37 = _____

   c. 0.265 + 0.333 = _____

   d. 0.625 – 0.5 = _____

   e. 0.725 – 0.62 = _____

   f. 0.385 + 0.615 = _____

   g. 1.627 + 2.3 = _____

   h. 1.258 – 0.255 = _____

   i. 0.925 – 0.638 = _____

   j. 3.645 + 2.895 = _____

   k. 0.875 – 0.055 = _____

   l. 0.427 – 0.355 = _____

1. Alex has £2.37 in his pocket and £1.85 in his hand.

   He can't work out how much he has altogether.

   Use a written calculation to show how much money Alex has altogether.

2. **a.** Which calculation helps you to solve the subtraction 0.562 – 0.387 = ?

   Circle it.

   0.562 + 0.387 = 0.949   0.949 – 0.562 = 0.387

   0.387 + 0.175 = 0.562   0.387 – 0.175 = 0.212

   b. Now write the answer: _____

3. A chef has 0.263g of salt and 0.175g of pepper.

   a. How much more salt than pepper does she have?

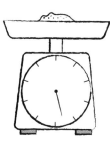

   _____ g

   Next, she mixes the salt and pepper together, and then puts 0.31g of the mixture into a saucepan.

   b. How much of the mixture will be left over?

   _____ g

10 Multiplying and dividing decimals

⟲ **Recap**

We organise numbers in power of ten.

So, in the number 3852.149, each digit represents a different power of ten.

thousands	hundreds	tens	ones	tenths	hundredths	thousandths
3	8	5	2	1	4	9

When we looked at fraction and decimal equivalence, we saw that

$3 \div 10 = 0.3$ $43 \div 100 = 0.43$ $743 \div 1000 = 0.743$

Notice how the digits move the same number of places as the power of ten dividing into it, for example:

$743 \div 1000$ the digits move three places to the right because 1000 is 10 to the power of three.

Remember: 1 tenth means $\frac{1}{10}$ or **1 divided by 10**, and so on.

📄 **Learn**

Just as we can divide by 10, 100 or 1000, we can multiply decimals by power of ten too.

$5.652 \times 10 = 56.52$ $5.652 \times 100 = 565.2$ $5.652 \times 1000 = 5652.0$

And, of course, we can multiply and divide decimals by other numbers.

We do this using the usual methods.

$$\begin{array}{r} 2.56 \\ \times \quad 3 \\ \hline 7.68 \\ {\scriptstyle 1 \quad 1} \end{array}$$

Notice how the digits move from right to left with multiplication.

$$4 \overline{)2.{}^2 5 {}^1 8 {}^2 0} \quad 0.645$$

Look at how we carry over the same for decimals as we do for whole number calculations.

✔ **Practice**

1. Multiply these decimals by whole numbers.

   a. $10 \times 0.5 =$ _____

   b. $10 \times 0.25 =$ _____

   c. $10 \times 0.725 =$ _____

   d. $100 \times 0.52 =$ _____

   e. $100 \times 0.372 =$ _____

   f. $100 \times 0.085 =$ _____

   g. $1000 \times 0.375 =$ _____

   h. $1000 \times 0.507 =$ _____

   i. $1000 \times 0.004 =$ _____

   j. $2 \times 0.3 =$ _____

   k. $3 \times 1.5 =$ _____

   l. $20 \times 3.6 =$ _____

2. Divide these numbers.

   a. $7 \div 10 =$ _____

   b. $0.4 \div 10 =$ _____

   c. $0.125 \div 10 =$ _____

   d. $16 \div 100 =$ _____

   e. $12.5 \div 100 =$ _____

   f. $379 \div 100 =$ _____

   g. $258 \div 1000 =$ _____

   h. $756 \div 1000 =$ _____

   i. $2784 \div 1000 =$ _____

   j. $9 \div 2 =$ _____

   k. $11 \div 5 =$ _____

   l. $9 \div 8 =$ _____

3. Find the answers.

   a. $0.3 \times 50 =$ _____

   b. $7 \times 0.12 =$ _____

   c. $67 \div 100 =$ _____

   d. $735 \div 10 =$ _____

   e. $3 \times 5.4 =$ _____

   f. $5 \times 3.26 =$ _____

   g. $100 \times 0.003 =$ _____

   h. $7 \times 6.04 =$ _____

   i. $15 \div 6 =$ _____

   j. $0.725 \times 8 =$ _____

   k. $19 \div 8 =$ _____

   l. $45 \div 200 =$ _____

⚠ Solve problems

1. Circle the calculation with the larger answer.

$$2564 \div 100 \qquad 2.564 \times 100$$

2. Write the missing numbers on each line.

   $7.5 \times$ _____ $= 75$ 　　　　　 $7.5 \div$ _____ $= 0.075$

   $7.5 \div$ _____ $= 0.75$ 　　　　　 $7.5 \times$ _____ $= 7500$

3. If six identical pencils weigh 192.24 grams, calculate the mass of a single pencil.

   _____ g

4. A builder has 50 identical wooden planks. Each plank is 1.242m long.

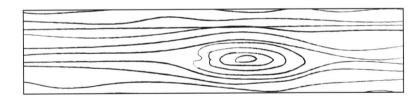

   How long would all the planks be when joined end to end?

   _____ m

11 Fraction, decimal and percentage equivalence

⟳ **Recap**

Fractions show a proportion of a quantity.

$\frac{3}{8}$ means three out of every eight.

For example, in a bag of 16 counters, three out of every eight are red, so altogether there will be six red counters.

Fractions with denominators of 10, 100 and 1000 can be easily changed to decimals.

$$\frac{47}{10} = 4.7 \qquad \frac{47}{100} = 0.47 \qquad \frac{47}{1000} = 0.047$$

📄 **Learn**

The word 'per cent' means for every 100 (per is 'for', cent is '100').

So, a fraction expressed with a denominator of 100 can be read as a **percentage**.

$\frac{47}{100} = 47\%$ Notice the percentage sign – % – we say 47 per cent.

So, we have fraction, decimal and percentage equivalence.

$\frac{47}{100} = 0.47 = 47\%$ They all have the same value!

To change any fraction to a percentage, you can either change the denominator to 100, or calculate the decimal equivalent.

$\frac{12}{20} = \frac{12}{20} \begin{smallmatrix} \times 5 \\ \times 5 \end{smallmatrix} = \frac{60}{100}$ or $12 \div 20 = 0.6$ Either way, it equals 60%!

1. Find the percentage equivalent for each decimal.

   a. 0.43 = _____

   b. 0.89 = _____

   c. 0.17 = _____

   d. 0.52 = _____

   e. 0.3 = _____

   f. 0.08 = _____

   g. 0.01 = _____

   h. 0.5 = _____

2. Find the equivalent percentage for each fraction.

   a. $\frac{13}{100}$ = _____

   b. $\frac{25}{100}$ = _____

   c. $\frac{72}{100}$ = _____

   d. $\frac{4}{100}$ = _____

   e. $\frac{37}{50}$ = _____

   f. $\frac{11}{20}$ = _____

   g. $\frac{7}{10}$ = _____

   h. $\frac{17}{25}$ = _____

   i. $\frac{1}{2}$ = _____

   j. $\frac{2}{3}$ = _____

   k. $\frac{3}{4}$ = _____

   l. $\frac{5}{8}$ = _____

3. Complete the equivalence chart, writing the fractions in their simplest forms.

Percentage	Decimal	Fraction
50%		
25%		
75%		
20%		
40%		
60%		
80%		

⚠ Solve problems

1. Circle the numbers that are equivalent to $\frac{3}{5}$.

   $\frac{6}{10}$ 40%   0.6

          60%   0.35 $\frac{2}{3}$

2. 60% of all the children at a party are girls. What fraction of the children are boys?

   Possible answers include fraction, improper fraction, decimal.

3. Half of the beads in a bag are red, and one fifth are green. All of the other beads are blue.

   What percentage of the beads is blue?

4. Tina says, $\frac{13}{20} = 65\%$

   Explain why she is correct:

12 Using percentages

A percentage is a proportion out of 100.

It can be written as a fraction with a denominator of 100.

$$23\% = \frac{23}{100}$$

It can also be written as a decimal.

$$23\% = 0.23$$

These numbers are all equivalent: $23\% = \frac{23}{100} = 0.23$

100% is equivalent to one whole.

📄 Learn

We can calculate percentages of quantities.

For example, if a baker has 12 bread rolls and sells 50% of them, how many does she have left?

We can say that 12 loaves is the whole amount: 100%.

We know that 50% is equivalent to one half, so half of the loaves have been sold, and therefore there must be 6 loaves left.

For harder calculations, such as 15% of 240, there are different approaches.

We can calculate $\frac{15}{100} \times 240$ ($15 \div 100 = 0.15$ then $0.15 \times 240 = 36$)

Or we can do it this way:

240 is 100%, so 10% = 24 (240 ÷ 10) and so 5% must be 12.

15% = 10% + 5%

So 15% of 240 = 24 + 12 = 36

1. What percentage of each set of dots is shaded?

a. 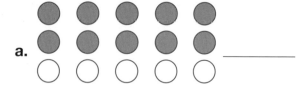 _____

b. 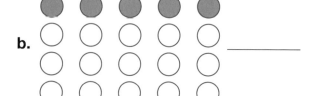 _____

c.  _____

d.  _____

e. 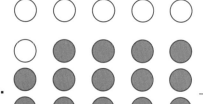 _____

f. 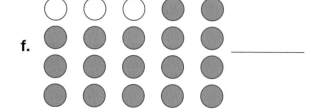 _____

2. Calculate these percentages.

   a. 50% of 20 = _____
   b. 10% of 20 = _____

   c. 60% of 20 = _____
   d. 50% of 30 = _____

   e. 10% of 30 = _____
   f. 70% of 50 = _____

   g. 80% of 50 = _____
   h. 1% of 200 = _____

   i. 15% of 200 = _____
   j. 31% of 200 = _____

3. Fill in the missing percentages.

   a. _____% of 10 = 5
   b. _____% of 10 = 1

   c. _____% of 10 = 8
   d. _____% of 40 = 20

   e. _____% of 40 = 4
   f. _____% of 40 = 30

   g. _____% of 10 = 7.5
   h. _____% of 300 = 30

   i. _____% of 300 = 270
   j. _____% of 300 = 45

⚠ Solve problems

1. A teacher has to pay 20% tax on the money she is paid for her work.

    If she is paid £2000, how much tax will she pay?

2. A sale in a computer shop has **15% off** all its laptops.

    Calculate the sale prices for each laptop.

Laptop name	Usual price	Sale price
Zing-a-ling	£500	
Rapido	£800	
Boggler	£900	
Zippy	£1200	

3. There are 650 children in a school.

    70% of the children have school dinners, 2% go home for lunch, and the rest bring packed lunches.

    Calculate how many children have each type of lunch.

    _____ school dinners _____ go home _____ packed lunches

Marks

There are 20 questions in total, one mark per question.
Try to do the test in one sitting of 20 minutes.

1. $\frac{3}{7} + \frac{2}{7} =$

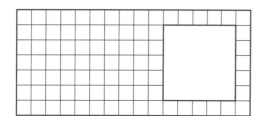

2. $3.4 - 0.7 =$

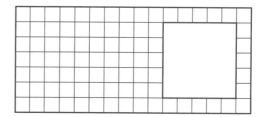

3. $\frac{45}{50} - \frac{22}{50} =$

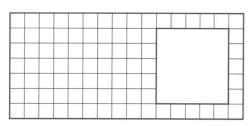

4. $\frac{3}{10} + \frac{2}{5} =$

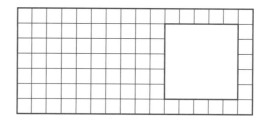

5. $7.83 + 1.2 =$

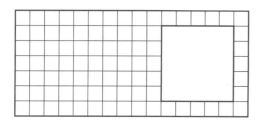

6. 20% of 150 =

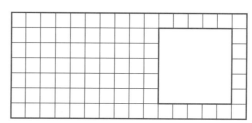

7. $0.75 \div 10 =$

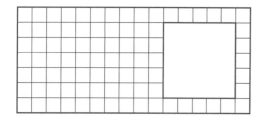

8. $23 - 11.85 =$

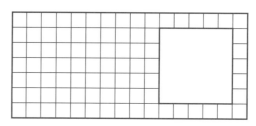

9. $0.73 \times 100 =$

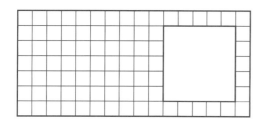

10. $\frac{6}{7} \div 3 =$

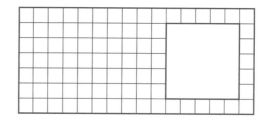

10

11. $\frac{1}{5} + \frac{1}{10} + \frac{1}{15} =$

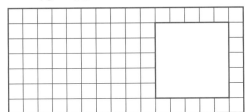

12. $\frac{2}{3}$ of 540 =

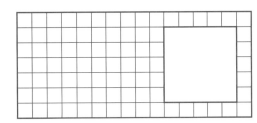

13. $3\frac{2}{5} + 2\frac{1}{4}$

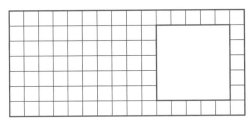

14. $21 \div 1000 =$

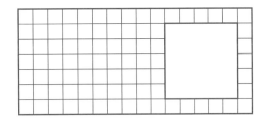

15. 7% of 600 =

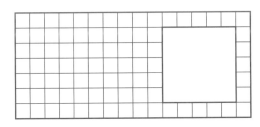

16. $\frac{3}{4} - \frac{1}{6} =$

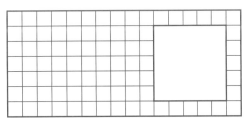

17. $3.25 \times 5 =$

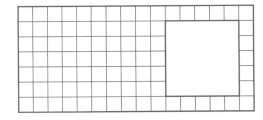

18. $2\frac{1}{4} \times 120 =$

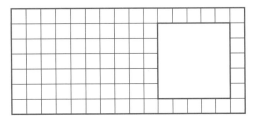

19. $0.8 \times 200 =$

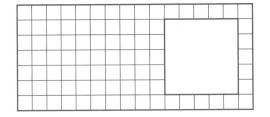

20. $\frac{1}{3}$ of $6\frac{1}{2} =$

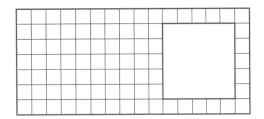

10

Marks

There are eight questions in total.

Try to do the test in one sitting of 15 to 20 minutes.

1. Write these decimals in order, from smallest to largest:

    0.613   0.361   1.630   0.163   3.016   0.316

    _____ _____ _____ _____ _____ _____

    smallest   largest

    1

2. Draw lines to the fraction to connect shapes that have $\frac{2}{3}$ shaded.

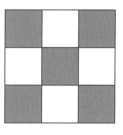
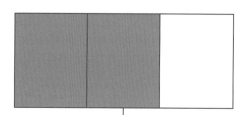
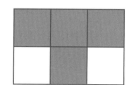

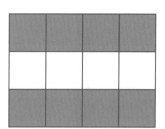
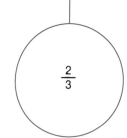
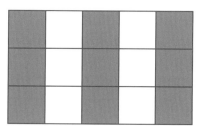

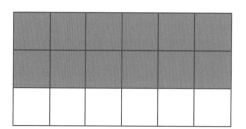

1

3. What number will make both these calculations correct?

$2 \div \boxed{?} = 0.002$

$0.402 \times \boxed{?} = 402$

4. A garden is 3m wide by 5m long.

PATIO	FLOWERBED
PATH	

If the patio is 2m by 2m, what fraction of the garden does the flowerbed cover?

Give the fraction in its simplest form.

5. Write the correct signs in each box. >, < or =.

$\frac{7}{14}$ ☐ $\frac{2}{3}$ $\frac{14}{7}$ ☐ $\frac{3}{2}$

$\frac{2}{7}$ ☐ $\frac{3}{14}$ $\frac{7}{2}$ ☐ $\frac{14}{3}$

1

6. Sugar is sold in bags of 1.75kg.

A box holds 60 bags of sugar.

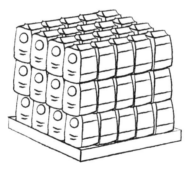

A supermarket received five boxes of sugar.

What will the total mass of the sugar be?

☐ kg

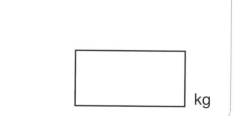

2

7. A factory makes buttons.

   Each week 6% of the buttons are damaged, and have to be destroyed.

   One week, 1356 buttons were destroyed.

   How many buttons were made altogether?

   buttons

   2

8. Yusef says the answer to this calculation is less than zero.

$$2\frac{1}{3} + 3\frac{3}{5} - 5\frac{7}{10}$$

   Explain why he is correct.

   _____

   _____

   _____

   1

Glossary

D

Decimal A fraction of a whole number shown in tenths, hundredths and thousandths. This is written using a decimal point.

0.125: Zero point one two five has one tenth, two hundredths and five thousandths.

Denominator The bottom number of a fraction showing how many parts the whole has been divided into.

$\frac{1}{3}$*: One third has a denominator of three.*

E

Equivalent Fractions, decimals and percentages that have the same value are equivalent.

$\frac{1}{4}$ = 0.25 = 25%*: One quarter is equivalent to zero point two five or 25 per cent.*

F

Factor A number that divides into another number. We use these to simplify fractions.

$\frac{2}{6} = \frac{1}{3}$*: Two and six have two as a common factor. It can be simplified to one third.*

Fraction One number divided by another to show part of a whole.

$\frac{3}{7}$*: Three sevenths is three out of seven equal parts of a whole.*

H

Highest common factor (HCF) The highest possible number that will divide into two different numbers.

The HCF of 12 and 15 is 3; the HCF of 20 and 30 is 10.

Sometimes the HCF can be one of the numbers. For example:

The HCF of 3 and 6 is 3.

I

Improper fraction A fraction with a numerator larger than its denominator.

$\frac{11}{5}$

This can also be written as a **mixed number**.

L

Lowest common multiple (LCM) The smallest number that two smaller numbers will divide into.

The LCM of 3 and 4 is 12.
The LCM of 6 and 8 is 24.

Sometimes the LCM can be one of the numbers. For example:

LCM of 2 and 4 is 4.

M

Mixed number A whole number and a fraction.

$2\frac{1}{5}$*: Two and one fifth represents two wholes and one fifth of a whole.*

Multiple A number made by multiplying two numbers together.

6 is a multiple of 2 and 3. (It is also a multiple of 1 and 6). 1, 2, 3 and 6 are all factors of 6.

N

Numerator The top number of a fraction showing the number of parts of a whole.

$\frac{1}{3}$*: One third has a numerator of one.*

P

Percentage The proportion of a quantity when divided into 100 equal parts.

75%: 75 per cent means 75 out of every 100.

Proportion The fraction used to represent an amount.

$\frac{1}{3}$ *of people own a pet.*
We can also say one in every three people, or one out of every three people, owns a pet.

S

Simplify To express a fraction in its simplest form.

Three twelfths $\frac{3}{12}$ *can be simplified as one quarter* $\frac{1}{4}$*.*